A Quarter Turn

Debra Nystrom

The Sheep Meadow Press
Riverdale-on-Hudson, New York

All inquiries and permission requests should be addressed to: The Sheep Meadow Press, P.O. Box 1345, Riverdale-on-Hudson, New York 10471.

Distributed by Consortium Book Sales & Distribution, Inc.
213 East 4th Street
St. Paul, MN 55101

Typesetting by Keystrokes, Lenox, Massachusetts
The book was composed in Mergenthaler Bembo

Library of Congress Cataloging-in-Publication Data

Nystrom, Debra.
    A quarter turn / Debra Nystrom.
      p.   cm.
    Poems.
    ISBN 1-878818-02-3. —ISBN 1-878818-00-7 (pbk.)
    I. Title.
    PS3564.Y78Q37   1991
    811'.54—dc20   90-26317
                                                                        CIP

Printed in the United States of America

for my teachers

ACKNOWLEDGMENTS

Thanks to the editors of the following magazines, in which these poems first appeared:

The American Poetry Review: A Worn Stairway; Bridge in Florence, in the Rain; Flooded Breaks; Late March; Passenger; With You Gone; Ordinary Heartbreak; Poem for a Bad Heart; The Puzzle

The Boston Review: Emily's Ghost, Human

The Denver Quarterly: Bellini's Madonna of San Giobbe

Five Fingers Review: Black and White Snapshot

Iris: Round

The Missouri Review: Flagstop

Ploughshares: A Quarter Turn (first published under the title A Game); Bonin Drowned; Five-Thirty, Driving Home; Reading Late; The Viewer

Prairie Schooner: Insomnia

Raccoon: Prairie Wind

Seneca Review: Eurydice; Kayleen; Leaving Dakota

The Seattle Review: Lying at Pancake Falls

The Threepenny Review: The Dream of Burning; Relic

TriQuarterly: Puppets; Wordless Hour; Cottage Above the Harbor; January Half-Light

The Virginia Quarterly Review: Parting; Silk; To Janny; The Faithless; At Ocracoke

Thanks also to Yaddo, The University of Virginia, and The Virginia Commission for the Arts for their support during the time I worked on this book.

And for their help with the manuscript version of the book, deepest gratitude to Juanita Brunk, Robert Pinsky, David Rivard, Ellen Bryant Voigt, Renate Wood, and especially Michael Ryan.

CONTENTS

A quarter turn, one more,
And there you are facing evening.

—Marie Luise Kaschnitz
"Toward Evening"

A QUARTER TURN

SILK

Typing paper and white-out bought, sacked,
and clutched to my breast as if with purpose,
I find myself still shopping: is it the wish to be,
or the feeling of being already no one at all
that lures me through the aisles and aisles of racks
of useless skirts, coats, scarves, and into the little
triple-mirrored, locked and hot-lit fitting stalls?
Work done for the week, not much appetite, so easy
to think—as the advertisers mock—why not
just try this silk? And it's the salesgirl's job
to seem to have all evening, to seem to know
your taste and know too that this dress she's brought you
you would never buy or even have occasion for,
but ought to: not sexy, necessarily; elegant in a way
meant to please nobody. You slip it over your everyday
cotton underwear and step out shyly. "Your color,"
she says, of course, buttoning the cuffs for you,
but then so gently turning you toward each mirror
with the cool shining fabric between you,
with her hands pressing your shoulders lightly,
not letting go.

RELIC

Iᴛ must've been some occasion—
the Granddad's birthday, maybe—
because all the family,
brothers, cousins, wives and kids,
took the afternoon fishing at the reservoir
that now covered the southwest quarter.
Years back he and his boys had been warned
of the planned flooding, had cashed
the Feds' check issued for their land,
then watched from their tractors
as hundreds of trucked-in workers in fancy rigs
shifted the bluffs year by year
till the massive earthen dam altered
even the weather, and bred mosquitoes there.
Grandma died a month before the first fields
went under, and just once the old man snapped
he was glad she didn't see it;
as little was said afterward of the lost land
as of her. Now the men baited lines
for the boys to cast, children waded
where the women could see them,
sandwiches and tea were unpacked,
pike after glittering pike was reeled in.
The treeless bank continued its quiet surrender
to the reservoir, unremarked,
and late in the afternoon one of the little ones
dredged up from the sand between her toes
a perfect rose quartz arrowhead
they passed from hand to hand.

PRAIRIE WIND

PIGEON wings shatter the sunlight
as my father rolls the barn door shut
behind him. His shirt-back billows.
He's hauling pails of milk across the ground.
The pigeons shimmer above, then vanish
as the blare of hot wind absorbs all sound.
Guineas scream from the granary eaves,
sheet metal quivers on a pile of junk machinery,
but he keeps walking, looking straight ahead of him,
hearing only millions of bits of land tear
from the farm. I climb down the loft-ladder,
hook the barn door's inside latch, then brush
the little side door shut across the dirt;
brush out the heat, the flapping shirt,
and unlash the rope so it hangs free
from the middle beam. The cows nod and I ride
toward first one wall, then another:
slamming at the boards with bare feet,
slamming against the howl outside
that wants to scatter us all,
warning it.

BELLINI'S MADONNA OF SAN GIOBBE
—Museo Accademia, Venice

It was a vague desire, I was so young
and in such ignorance, but the way
her face lifts at the chin just
slightly, turns as slightly to the left
and stares above the head of her infant son
past saints gathered around her,
beyond the random museum visitors
into another air, hand raised in recognition
of the perfect note she seems to hear—
I wanted this. In third grade I thought
it was hidden in the open baluster.

I forgot that first week Sunday school
was switched to meet an hour later;
got dropped off hurriedly at the usual time.
The organist practiced upstairs,
thinking herself alone, and as her hymn chords boomed
I wandered the unlit lower floor,
curtain to heavy velvet curtain,
fingering everything: robes, chalices, beads, lace,
and then the hollow baluster in the corner staircase,
whose square fitted cover had come loose.
I thrust my arm in
and ran my palm along the rough unfinished inside
I couldn't see or reach the bottom of, or divulge
even to myself, until, years later,
laughing that it had contained nothing,
I took a boy up in the choir loft to heighten
making-out with the thrill of blasphemy.

Once in a dream I found, at the bottom
inside the baluster, a lake
surrounded by ocean-smoothed stones

and still as a cautious animal—
a deer, watching, letting you near,
braced to disappear.
But I forgot my belief and disappointment both,
and had forgotten the baluster entirely
until turning here, in a corridor twenty years
and six thousand miles away, to find her:
more gorgeous than any Titian Venus, yet wearing
that same sublime, forbidden flush,
and these eyes—no heart-stopping color, but as though
she gazes out from behind a film of water.

RESTLESS AFTER SCHOOL

Nothing to do but scuff down
the graveyard road behind the playground,
past the name-stones lined up in rows
beneath their guardian pines,
on out into the long, low waves of plains
that dissolved time. We'd angle off
from fence and telephone line, through
ribbon-grass that closed behind as though
we'd never been, and drift toward the bluff
above the river-bend where the junked pick-up
moored with its load of locust skeletons.
Stretched across the blistered hood,
we let our dresses catch the wind
while clouds above us dimmed their tinge—
pink to purple to blue-and-shadow—
kindling our skin, then cooling it
so slow, as if we listened
to our own bones grow.

PUPPETS

Legs crossed, derrière perched daintily
on the corner of her desk, Mrs. Twitchell
reads aloud from the *Brittanica*
a history of papier-maché,

her half-moon glasses aimed toward the page
and not the kids whose hands are shiny gray
with the novel glee of newsprint strips
and flour-water paste. At their age

the past is meaningless; here and now
absorbs them: wrapping goopy strips
around light bulbs brought from home.
But some envision little gowns

they'll sew to hide their hands beneath,
and a few already plan the props
and headgear (magician's wand and cap; a crown;
one girl, obsessed with Jackie Kennedy's grief,

will top her light bulb with a pillbox hat).
At the rear three boys slop paper on,
bored with puppets, racing one another
and scheming out of Mrs. Twit's earshot,

impatient for the paste to dry
so they can bash the inside glass
to rattle like maracas. Others smoothe
layer after layer hypnotically:

this one the way her father strokes her hair;
this other, turned aside, not once looking up,

as if it's himself he re-constructs
around the hollow core,

the way at home he pretends he has no real
body, that inside the fleshy sham
of face and butt and limbs that can be smacked
anytime, he's nothing, untouchable.

CAPTIVE

In the evening when my dad pulled his hat off
his forehead looked soft where it was usually covered,
above the line where the rough tan stopped.
Sometimes he took me along at dusk
in the pick-up, while he closed pasture gates
and checked the cattle, and looked out
across the wheat to the west for the weather.
Maybe I'd ask a question about birds, and he'd answer,
but he seemed alone, driving out,
bumping over the fields to a spot just to look beyond it.

On the road to Uncle Norman's stood that old dying house
—it must be gone by this time—
the porch was torn from the second story, and someone
could've walked right out into the air.
Almost every Sunday we rode past it, and I imagined
a young man held captive there
by the high grass and wind. Once when I asked
Dad stopped the car so I could look in: some pigeons
suddenly flew out; inside, between the boards of the walls,
thin cracks of light.

Whole afternoons while the horses sauntered and chewed
I'd scoot along the corral-rails, trying
to make it all the way around without touching ground.
Walking beyond the wind-break I used to think
the rest of the world must look like that,
bleached dry and flat.
Wherever you turned
you could see the circle of horizon
as the meadowlark repeated
four notes to the unbroken sky.

BONIN DROWNED

Today I would like nothing
but the quick, violent breaking
of this storm that's crossed the plain
from the west all day, reminding me
of my schoolfriend Brenda's dad, Bonin.
The *Pierre Gazette* featured a photo
of the boat found below the dam, wrecked,
and Brenda must've known that week
how matter-of-factly the phrase
Bonin Drowned was read.
But maybe it wasn't foolishness
or the accident dealt
for being a drunk; maybe
he had simply spent another mute,
indifferent day of the kind
that go on there for months,
and despite warmth, comfort, lack
of irritation, he could think finally
of no hope, no threat,
no touch from wife or daughter,
nothing that would put aside the wish
to be taken by the water
and taken from himself by force.

EPITHALAMIUM

W E had moved in before we learned
that down the hill on the interstate
maybe a hundred rigs a night
heave past with their sealed freight

in monstrous arhythmic waves
we hear from inside our dreams:
waves bellying out of black silence
as if to dash us from the room.

Some nights rain changes the waves to sheets
of slick, heavy fabric torn and torn and torn.
If we ever see behind what's ripped away,
will we learn to love it in each other's arms?

FIVE-THIRTY, DRIVING HOME

THE swallows rush, shadowless,
through evening's thick, sweet light
—color of honey, color
of the pine of our paneled ceiling,
beneath which I drowse too soon,
beneath which I wake at dawn
unable to recall my dreams,
and lie for my five minutes
staring at the pine's knots,
hurling the mind's useless hatchet
at the dark targets sanded flat.
To one side you sleep, hand open;
to the other the black aspen
takes shape in the window again.
What is it that angers me then?
I have home, I have love—
still, the light I see by is never
daylight, never the clarity
that signals the hawk's flight,
who views not simply grasses
but the slightest movements beneath,
and seizes precisely what he needs—
while fox and coyote hunt
by watching that high, lone circling.

LEGACY
—H.V.S., 1899–1986

So unlikely to have lasted
a lifetime on the prairie,
these turn-of-the-century toys
she left to me: an egg basket
for one egg only; the china doll
in calico I remember her calling Beulah;
and this glass pistol not ever broken
for the red and white pellet candies,
faded now, still trapped inside.

READING LATE

The Heart wants what it wants—
or else it does not care—
                    —Emily Dickinson

So still. Not a cricket. In this heat
the trees around the house hold motionless
even at midnight. I trundle the electric fan,
little pool of wind, along with me
from room to room, and imagine Emily Dickinson
carrying a candle that defines her sphere
into a part of the house where she won't hear
her sister Vinnie start to snore.
Just now, while you're gone, I wouldn't
have to be reading her,
who closed herself in with her wild need
and the deprivation by which she meant
to know, wholly, her desire. No one ever
will figure out how much it was a wish
for someone in particular—Reverend Wadsworth,
maybe, her deep-voiced "Dusk Gem"—
and how much it was a longing that had no object
but oblivion, which allows no interruption.

THE VIEWER

AND a feature about the only son
of the famous "Angel of Death"
who experimented at Auschwitz:
I fold the section once in half
and then in half again, as if
to narrow focus, but glimpse instead
a lizard as it shoots up the steps outside
then vanishes behind the photos and postcards
lined up against my closed window.
The son, born in 1944, saw
nothing of the war's horrors,
and nearly as little of his father
these forty years. But the violated strangers—
old film clips, faces from bad dreams—
how intimately must he know them?
I recall from yesterday's *Science Section*
that the human brain can store
ten thousand faces in memory, or more.
Now they think they've found
not the long-sought face,
but the bones of Doctor Mengele.
And into all this sifts the Sixties' movie
I watched for half-price Saturday:
a guy smuggling two ki's of skag
back from Nam, terrified,
feeling for the first time in his life
he's really doing something.
That same actor played a spineless Nazi
with the same broad forehead ten years ago
on TV. So I process history.
Out on the porch the lizard flicks again,
and across the highway the rummage sale
outside the Crossroads Store, where daily

I buy my trucked-in *Times,* is over.
Poor people finish selling junk to one another
and pack up their cars. Faces—
already I remember none of theirs, as I look
at my pictures of pictures on the sill:
open-mouthed Medusa, Cranach's
hard-eyed Eve, the head of Mary
held by two anonymous
hands of mercy.

A QUARTER TURN

It was a way to toy with the warning
against playing in the woods at evening:
they would all coast down the three-block hill
with their legs tucked and soles flat on the seats,
then leap where the road ends abruptly at the pines
whose branches are so heavy, it seems
their own volition and not the wind that moves them.
Last night the first one tore in after his bike
and found a dead woman next to it: breasts,
thighs and face smeared with red, wrists tied
to a trunk with flowered shreds of her dress.
He stared for a minute before flailing out,
and for those hours he might've spent with his family
or in front of the TV, he talked to police.
His friends will no doubt think of another game,
but tonight after dinner the boy comes up to his room
to watch from the window until there is nothing
beyond the streetlights' clear domain.

ORDINARY HEARTBREAK

S<small>HE</small> climbs easily onto the box
that seats her above the swivel chair, at adult
height, crosses her legs, left ankle over right,
and smoothes the plastic apron over her lap while
the beautician lifts her ponytail and remarks,
"Coarse as a horse's tail."

Then as though that's all there is to say,
the woman at once whacks off and tosses
its foot-and-a-half into the trash;
and the little girl who didn't want her hair cut
but long ago learned how not to say
what it is she wants,

who even at this minute can not quite grasp
her shock and grief, *is* getting her hair cut,
"for convenience," her mother put it—
the long waves gone that had been evidence
at night, when loosened from their clasp,
she might be secretly a princess.

Rather than cry out, she grips her own wrist
and looks to her mother in the mirror,
but her mother is too polite or too reserved or
too indifferent to notice any signal.
So the girl herself takes up indifference,
while hurt follows a hidden channel

to a place unknown to her, convinced
as she is that her own emotions
are not the ones her life depends on.
She shifts her gaze from her mother's face
back to the haircut now, so steadily, as if
this short-haired child she sees were someone else.

INSOMNIA

It's the ceaseless wind
off the prairie, blasting
grit into the window casings,
snapping one brittle weed against
the pane, rousing rattlesnakes—
blinded in this season
of shedding skins, they will strike
at any vibration.

Try to lie without moving,
think nothing, sink,
follow the exposed poplar roots
that crowd to the lip
of the cistern's cool, cement lid:
within, broader than
a man's arm-span, three times deeper
than his height, the wet dark
of the slick-sided cylinder
does not admit wind
or snake. But I am too weak
to lift the lid alone.

FLOODED BREAKS

I remember drowsiness, the cloudy heat,
the familiar mixed smells of our sweat, even
the pressure of my cheekbone against the front seat
and the sense of promptly forgetting a thing
you had just told me. Suddenly
after hours of talk and dust and ragged plain
we reached the Missouri's thick, unadorned curve:
rush of water looking muscular from above
and denser than the land there, which seemed
translucent for its lack of color,
as if the swallows plunging toward the cliff
might pass through it.
We drove on, but shining for a second below,
rising from the current where the bank had once been,
the tops of trees wavered, stripped and whitened.
More trees would appear in time
to line the river's new edge, but what we saw
had the gorgeous starkness of a place forsaken,
as if our glimpse of it would be the last.

LATE MARCH

THE geese are flying north along the river again,
searching the brittle fields for grain.
In the middle of the night I feel your hand on me,
and lie still.

I want to hear the geese, is all—
the dark calling for spring.
I want to go to the window and look for the moon,
thinking of no one.

The river breaks and then freezes, breaks and freezes,
trying to move.
What does it need from the birds
that follow it home?

BLACK AND WHITE SNAPSHOT

I don't remember the party; I remember
getting ready, when Grandma, who nightly
cupped me in bed in her flannel lap,
grabbed from me the flat white brassiere
and threw it to the floor.
How I gathered my clothes up one by one,
walked evenly to the bathroom,
locked the door, stepped calf-deep
into water, pulled my housecoat off.

I lay still there. Leaves fluttered
at the window's dull square like tickling,
like ruffles on the swimsuit I wore
when I was little and Dad would carry me
on his back underwater; and I began trailing
through the bath around my clean body
the red washcloth that spread itself
gracefully as a jellyfish, animal
that stings what touches it.

My father posed me before those woods
in my starched dress, steadying my shoulders
between his hands. The shoulders
and white skirt keep me apart from the forest,
but look at the face, look at the curve
my neck makes toward the pine's textured trunk
that rises from the same decayed bed of ferns
I stand upon and will return to
alone and lie down.

TO KEITH
(1954–1972)

In my dream you're waiting on the street,
idling outside the Lariat Cafe while I
count my tips and put the ketchups away—
you're leaning out of that
jacked-up pink chevy we'd bolt town in
to tune in the rock from Oklahoma City
and skim along moon-dim back roads,
going nowhere. You raise your arm to me,
the one with the hand cut off, though that's not
the way you did it. You pulled the chevy
into the YOU-WASH-IT after school,
rolled both hinged doors down to the concrete
and slid back in behind the wheel,
radio up, motor roaring.
But in the dream you're still waiting for me,
your old girlfriend, the one
you gave your diaries to that day
—and I didn't ask why, though we weren't
going together anymore; I didn't ask,
didn't even look before
I stuffed them in my locker at lunch;
I liked being the keeper of feelings,
being needed but not touched.

LEAVING DAKOTA

Do the prairie-winters breed this silence
we've learned to need?
There must be prairies in Sweden.
The Nystroms pressed into America
two thousand miles for empty land,

and not an inch south. When the old man died
Great Grandma travelled back
to Sweden to find his brother,
then returned with him her second husband
to the same sod house.

Five months inside waiting out
ice-winds held off by no hills, no trees,
as the miles between the farms increase;
the stark intimacy of one room
survived with silence and fire.

So it comes from weather, this restraint?
Into my moment of goodbye, your broad face
looming, Father, the lines in your lips,
the gray-green eyes, suddenly:
our quick, shaking kiss.

WORDLESS HOUR

*L*OOK *at the lilac, vivid and dying*
in the honeysuckle's clench,
whose scent is sweeter yet.
—And the shadows they make together,
darkest in this heavy glare, this weight,
almost like rain on the air,
although the sky is clear. These things
I might have said from my lawn chair.
I might have said *Tell me about her.*
Or, *There isn't even anyone else, is there?*

Instead, *How about a movie tonight?*
—Since we long for war or strife
or intrigue, don't we,
to upstage the undramatic loss of love
to time and our own mistakes.
Now I tilt my head to fasten my earring
and see you waiting at the car
in the long rectangular beam the window throws
like a spotlight into the evening.
Somehow it makes you vaguer, though:
jacket flapping before the trees in motion,
the branches in the dusk at your back
entangling and dissolving.

PARTING

Nothing could have made it less abrupt—
not the next taxi instead, not a longer hug,
a placid rather than a drizzly sky;
nothing would have made you cry before
I was in, telling the driver where to take me,
and you loaded in my bag and closed the door
carefully, holding on an extra second
to the wet handle, then letting go

while through the streaked back window
I watched as long as possible
your shaking head, your one hand raised to me;
then watched the rainy blossoms
shaking on the trees; and then, beneath the trees,
other people on the streets—
some hurrying, some not; all of them,
all of them remote.

PASSENGER

ONLY when the train began pulling out from some town
I hadn't seen, did I wake from that long dream
of black waving lilies, cross my legs again,
and notice the boards of the platform
passing. And this girl,
this young woman still standing, still
looking for somebody as faces flickered by her blankly.
A simple felt cap in her hands, coat open,
the corner of it catching up as the train
forced the night air into motion; and I moved myself—
not her lover, not even a man—
desiring to abandon a half-remembered life,
to draw her mournful dark mouth toward my own.

HUMAN

Smooth, taut, warm breast
of a woman twenty-eight,
I wanted someone else to feel it.
And touching the comfort
of my own skin, in the dark,
under the sheet, I thought of that
old fat sightless man, for God's sake,
in his white crew cut. Because he
had been asking the same thing?
Years of unchecked syphilis
had blinded him. No medical record,
no family; he came in every week
to the optometrist's office where I worked
after school and Saturdays.
Said he had money for treatment,
and would pull out, to show me,
ones, fives, tens, twenties
folded in four different ways.
Sometimes he'd just linger in the waiting room
after hearing again that nothing
could be done. And I wondered
how he pictured my face—
if he thought everybody still looked like
those brooding people in lace and black
lined up shoulder to shoulder
in my grandparents' photographs.
How had he gotten it?
Someone he had loved? Someone
willing on a bad night?
Though according to the instruments
he couldn't distinguish the faintest light,

he kept his milky eyes open—
maybe in defiance, maybe to invite
assurance he was still human
as he listened to other patients
watching him over magazines,
turning pages touched by a hundred hands.

IN YOUR HOUSE

I saw plants straining to one side,
ragged and stiff in the living room,
as though they had waited a long time to turn
and bend another way for sunlight.

No pictures on the walls.
Just the walls. The house I used to live in
felt like yours: floors worn gray,
long spells of overcast days. I'd like

to lie beside you in a room
and look at the ceiling
and neither of us speak.

When did I live there? Not with husband
or father. A bare third floor,
windows open to clean rain;
no sound of anyone.

THE DREAM OF BURNING

—Villa of the Mysteries, Pompeii

They were not burned, but suffocated
by the time all color finally flared
beneath the black cloud and faded.
Yet this buried room—in blood-red,
gold, and purple—preserved the dream of burning,
dance of the body's furious wish,
arc of the whip slapped against itself.
Like water splashed and arrested,
figures lean their heads together, and whirl,
and bend for the lash of initiation.
A satyr stares at the augury inside a bowl;
a stiff-shouldered, naked boy—the youngest—
keeps his eyes on the page of some sacred text;
while the rest gaze from scene to scene at one another,
except for the veiled one alone in her corner by the door,
who seems, like me, rapt in the whole drama before her.
She—even more than Dionysius, who sprawls,
spent, in the center panel—she presides.
Or is she also the one with cymbals?
Or flinging her shawl up in alarm?
Or arranging her hair before a mirror,
preparing for what comes when, closing the eyes,
not only thought but even the body is forgotten?

EURYDICE

He stood before me stricken by the light
he thought I too had reached,
as the scent of pine bleeding in Thracian heat
entered the night corridor around me.
Behind, the reluctant arm of Hermes laced mine
already—how can *he* stand to witness it
again and again, that upper-world-terror of loss
searing the faces of the living?
He knew the first time the cry
that would pursue us as he drew me down.
Twice I have had to forget
the beauty of my husband's song,
but as long as that voice persists someplace
I cannot stop dying.

FLAGSTOP

SHADOW at a window stroking a white cat:
though the shadow and the angle of my view
hide all but a hand and indifferent animal,
I know you are female. The streets
and station return nothing for your vigil,
and I think you sit there nightly
receiving no touch—just a pressure of air
from the evening train's departure.
Oh, for all I know you thrive on longing.
Maybe you imagine gazing as I am
from a window of the train, and at once
recognizing by the change in his breathing
(as if you had lived years with him)
that the other passenger in the compartment
has drowsed off. You glance at his lips,
parted a bit, his limbs' slack strength,
hand hanging open, and feel the invitation
of a body emptied of future and past,
like those eyeless bronzes dredged from the Aegean
as if from a dream.
Do you brush his arm, or fingers, or just
shift a leg to lean against him?
Or simply wait for the train to shudder
and pull out again, so he'll wake to see you
rubbing your own bare arm, staring out
at a hand that pets a white cat
again and again? But by then it would matter
who he is, what he believes, what sort
of book it is lying beside him on the cushion,
and you would begin to notice
these trees blackening at the edge of town,
shapes that alter only by chance of wind
there's no compelling or predicting.

ROUND

Are you an old woman already? Had you
forgotten that sound? Girls. Girls singing—
voices impervious to disappointment—
probably from some religious school,
hiking to the monastery at the dead-end
up the hill, for a view of the city.
Blue jumpers, or plaid; blunt-cut hair—
how did they slip by?

From the north window, as usual,
nobody; to the south, only
the aproned landlady, bent over what must be
the season's first fuzz of weeds.

There was music, though—a kind of round—
Stop moping, they might have been singing in Italian
simply for the sounds on their tongues,
It won't bring you anyone.

Morning shadows exaggerate the curve
of the barn's roof, where the boards
have caved slowly inward from the peak.
The girls disappeared with their song
and their clapping, not caring, at least
for that moment, about a destination,
so entranced by the round
with which their voices bound them.

A WORN STAIRWAY

I didn't startle them. Several other people
strolled through the mist along the old granite river-wall,
and the couple didn't notice; but their two faces parted
as I crossed toward them, and hers was lost a moment
in the shadow below his chin. I heard her voice
as I passed: one sharp sound; two falling.
In the bar after that there was a foolish girl intent
on wedging between her boyfriend and the cute
pouting foreign thing he leaned to stare at.
And when I had shoved out to the street again, a shoeless woman
was chased through a gate and turned abruptly by the coat.
All night pain mocked itself like that.
So when partway down a hill the walled road curved and opened
on a stair whose ancient steps rose like waves
through mullein and alder, I heard the echo of my own retreat,
but thought for a moment you had come down to find me.

POEM FOR A BAD HEART

In Florence in winter those stone
churches are colder than the streets;
does the old caretaker-priest,
wrapped in his cassock and muffler,
sit this morning in the Santa Maria del Carmine,
shifting his chair hour by hour
with the light from the south window,
attentive for off-season tourists who call
"Masaccio?" with its comic echo?
Is he pointing them another time to the far front,
right of the altar, the Brancacci Chapel,
where Saint Peter still draws
the coin from the fish's mouth behind
scaffolds and nets and torn canvas flaps,
so that to see it they have to
lean uncomfortably left and press
their faces against a pipe?
And will they have the patience after this,
despite tourists' pique or a spat over breakfast,
to listen to the old man's apology,
his entreaty to return when the work
is finished, his wish that his own heart last
through the final restoration? Has anyone
known those Masaccios as he has,
the day-by-day dimming of Adam and Eve
as they howl out of Eden?
How will they finally look to him,
redeemed?

JANUARY HALF-LIGHT

Sunless, shadowless, dream-time,
ironing shirts by the window,
listening to the stereo play again

"My Foolish Heart" in Bill Evans'
drawn-out, plaintive alteration
that makes the notes mean

for once what they always wanted to.
Across the valley that I watched you
trudge down early in the afternoon

parasol pines sway as if the glassy sky
were almost water-density,
like half-lit smoke in a jazz club

where people across the room
seem to move weightlessly,
lifted and tipped by old mute wishes

the music returns them to.
The piano drifts, dips; the drums
tump on their own for a bit; someone

steps in from the forgotten cold
and stamps his boots. Steam rises
as I lift the iron and set it

on its end in sudden quiet,
turning to see if it's you there again,
in your damp coat.

BRIDGE IN FLORENCE, IN THE RAIN

THE crammed bus turned suddenly,
and she as well as the dingy ones
fell against one another, grabbing in all directions
to hang on somewhere. We had all been calm, idly
watching her, the platinum blonde
dressed in fur and polish, as in clear weather
one might meander toward the center of a park and stare
without thought at the bright reflecting pond.

Being a stranger there, I looked out to see what
had jostled us, and found in the glass not
the face whose crimson lips I'd been imitating
to myself, but the railing's
rusted lace, hanging above the river,
the Arno, rising darker than water, and thicker.

THE PUZZLE
5.27.89

Funny little object:
three blocks of wood attached
to turn both ways
on one another, so the heads
and bellies and feet
of four painted creatures
can be interchanged.
A pink pelican, for instance,
with fish flopping
in its bill, propped
on an iguana's scaled
haunches and striped tail,
though in the middle it's
a porcupine idly
twiddling its quills.
—But that leaves out
the anxious frog, who's
split up among the other
three puzzle-sides:
turn the thing and find him
spotting a bug, but stuck
without his hopping equipment.
Each permutation
I try once more, then
line the parts up properly,
thinking to send the toy
to Claudia, who's almost two
—or maybe four, as a gleam,
if you count the time
of her parents' longing.
I wonder if a two-year-old
will like the puzzle half

as much as I do. In truth
I didn't bring it home
as a gift for Claudia
to begin with. And how much
was it even meant
for our child, who disappeared
when we couldn't yet
feel movement
and needed a sign of what
might be? Now the frog,
even with its feet on right,
just gazes up to what it wants.
We shouldn't have kept it
waiting on the nightstand
like that.

CHILD STARING

The ancient bowl from Shanghai
tilted on its pedestal
is less a fragile treasure
than a tiny hemisphere of sky:

faint ceramic pinks and blues
interpenetrating cloudlike
and seeming to shift continuously
before the eyes of viewers

who don't all necessarily
catch their breath and stare
like this child halted in front of it—
after all, it's lasted centuries.

Now it lasts another minute,
and another, and the luminous-faced
girl with parted lips and eyes that
half widen, then half-squint, continues

for a minute to forget the books in her arms,
to reveal herself before strangers
drifting through the room, as if such
pure expression could prevent all harm.

TO JANNY
(1953–1984)

T HE highway stills a minute;
I can hear leaves simmering
in the wet heat, and, posed twice
before another truck shudders past,

the old question of the bob-white
—one note hesitant, one perplexed—
we used to imitate.
Nothing moves except the traffic

and a river-elm dragging its branches
a few inches across the grass
like a girl's long hair when the tire-swing
has come to rest and she tips her head far back.

HER WALK ALONG THE CREEK

I hate the smell. Always
I'll hate it. Pine: not woods,
but that farm-grubby bathroom.
The coarse, grease-cutting soap my uncle
made me use when he'd finished inside me.
I don't know how we never were missed
by anyone; don't know how to care
that someone must've done a thing
like it to him.

What hurts most, what
is nearly or completely forgotten—
does it have to be turned
into further hurt instead of something
new, something not wrong, but pure
like these ferns uncurling from rot
on the caved-in log? I take
another step: the quick, faint
shock of walking through a spider web.

—for C.F.

MAKING THE BED

THIS quilt is fading now
that my grandmother sent us
for our wedding three years ago.
And I have taken to lying awake
at night, making up dreams to tell you,

unable to find another way
to explain a sorrow that had nothing,
in the beginning, to do with you.
I know it's not you who robbed me
of the hope of intimacy.

I never tell you those fake dreams anyway;
they're just a trick
for easing myself into the dark.
When finally I sleep I half dream them,
half dream the uncontrollable things.

Last night it began with me
sitting in the shadow of a doorway,
stroking the hair of a small girl,
my daughter, I think, though not yours.
I had her look like me. Was it self-pity?

Then sleep brought in this huge
sexless character whose face I couldn't see;
whose intent, I knew, was to snatch
my daughter from me, and in truth
I feared not the child's harm, but being lonely.

What would Grandma say, who once knew
everything about me; who used to be the one
sleeping underneath the quilt with me?
Twenty years ago I quit
telling her anything, you see.

COTTAGE ABOVE THE HARBOR

Now, at dawn, back from the dock's brink
stumps a small blond boy with a bucket,
singing something to himself.
How did he first get to the end of the dock
without my seeing him walk out? And who
lets him wander here at this hour alone?

As though waiting myself for his return, I've
been pacing the porch-boards from corner to corner,
watching the shadowed masts tip back and forth
like indecisive compass needles, while inside
my husband sleeps on with his hand under his face,
trying to answer his separate restlessness.

I wish the boy would not turn left or right
when he steps on to the road, but come
straight ahead, singing his song
up to this house to steady us, as easily as
he steadies his bucket of unknown contents.
With one hand he does it.

AT OCRACOKE

This silver light could dissolve everything
into one substance. Already the borders
of sand and ocean and air are unclear,
and people down the beach glitter
and shift like bluish chips of jewels
washed in from some old shipwreck
and left to mix with the seaweed strips.

Even what's up close wears the blueness
of distance: a styrofoam cup; these half-sunk
slivers of fishbones; your dingy running shoes
dangling from the hand that swings, familiar,
beside me. So we walk, letting the cold foam
rush about our ankles and recede;
letting the waves take what talk might be

between us now, as though they could form some
answer to our longings. We split our attention
between the curving, fading line of shore
that we'd like to follow forever
and the beautiful broken shells
dropped at our feet by the water
to remind us to love our imperfect selves.

for Michael

EMILY'S GHOST

Sumac tassels shrivel at their tips,
the milkweed hulls have all cracked open—
only this one I've found with a few seeds left,
their fibers still waiting for the wind.

I push up a sleeve and blow them myself
down my bare arm
and one white veil snags in the ragged bouquet
that has my hand sweating and stinking of weed-balm:

Queen Anne's lace and these strange
prickly purple berries.
They make a lovely arrangement,
and as long as I have the bouquet to carry,

the trucks and pickups bumping by
flashing sun off their windshields into my eyes
should see no need to honk or hoot or pull over
to offer a ride. At least no need of mine.

LYING AT PANCAKE FALLS

P ERFECT spot, with the perfect slight
indentations. Hips, breasts, elbows, cheekbone—
my whole weight pressing into this hot
flat stone would've caused no suffering
and felt none, had it lain these years
just another stone slope,
sunlight and water braiding over it.
Across the layers of rock below
strands of creek separate, then recompose
their rivulet. All this is accident,
the force that guilt always wishes to rule out.
Yet the mind repeats its *please, please,* not
picturing his face any longer, but following one black
igneous streak through the granite
to home, to the funny little Dakota Museum
with its stuffed buffalo, gas-mask from World War Two,
skull discovered caging the flint head of an arrow.
Out front, unmarked, half-sunk
in the grass by the parking lot, lodged the prayer rock:
smoother than this one, leveled,
made beautiful by its long, grinding journey
beneath the glacier. The Sioux took it for its shape
and, long before the time of my Saturday visits,
had worn into its surface the inch-deep
impression of a hand that drew your own hand down.
There my own flesh and sweat and wrongdoing fit
where thousands like and unlike it
had been cradled by absolving, indifferent stone.

THE FAITHLESS

THESE evening hours of blank heat I feel
utterly alone, until the air ripples a bit
and I think of everyone luxuriating in its gift
at once, like a congregation. I live, after all,

in town, on a quiet street, in a building
of thirty apartments and at least
as many people, dulled like me, half-dressed,
idling near open windows or on landings.

The breeze with its vetch-and-dust scent
touches us all and then departs; how can we
not turn our faces away
from the screens, and discount it?

AFTER THE SERVICE

Who knows if Grandma Hazel believed
in any sort of god beyond the whims
of dust devils and thunderheads?
She went to church when taken: weddings,
funerals, obligations. But Mom, who seems
suddenly frailer, wearing her mother's
cloudy opal ring—Mom lived more years

in town: I could tell as a kid that she
believed she *should* believe. That did her
more harm than good, as far as I could see.
Each week I'd march myself to Sunday school
with my starched dirndl rocking, wanting
to be the little savior of the family,
to memorize right answers for everybody.

Tonight we talk late at the kitchen table,
Mom and I, neither of us saying we have
no hope to sleep. Now and then
her left hand turns the worn ring that must
be large for her. Now and then I put
my arm around her, tiny woman,
last shield against the questions.

WITH YOU GONE

—It wasn't the phone. Probably some
semi's hum out on the highway;
but your voice passed over me anyway, like wind,
as if to shake me from a dream.
I've sat these hours doing nothing, watching traffic
vanish down the darkening valley, drinking a little,
not suffering. In Agrigento we saw the carabinieri
drag a boy from a train by the jacket
pulled inside-out over his arms and head: three of them
banged him the length of the concrete platform,
while another yanked the girl screaming after them
back inside the compartment again.

These nights I get home, walk through every room
with my coat on, and think how the sun
has crossed your study another time,
bleaching pages left strewn
in the configuration of some thought you had.
Once from this window I saw you lift a hand
to the beech's smooth gray trunk, and tip your head
toward the yellow leaves brilliant with decay,
as if speaking to a woman I've never known.
If not by recklessness, we're damaged by caution,
you said. How could I love your life apart from mine?

THROUGH A WINDOW

O<small>NLY</small> one tree with any leaves
still hanging in the wind.
The others: stripped, quivering
in a sky that wavery blue
of glass too old and thick.
But then, quick, all
in a second or two,
a scatter of swallows

like the flash of minnows
under the surface
of a pond I came to
thirty years ago, following
the cow-path beyond the fenced draw
while no one at the house knew.
A glinting all at once;
gone. No other stir. No sound.

BIOGRAPHICAL NOTE

Debra Nystrom grew up in South Dakota. In 1980 she earned her MFA degree from the Goddard Writing Program in Vermont. She has been a Hoyns Fellow in Poetry at the University of Virginia and a recipient of a Virginia Commission for the Arts Prize. She lives in Charlottesville, Virginia and teaches at the University of Virginia.